Modernism rou
On the doors of
plaque marks km of the European Modernism Route.

KT-364-233

CASA BATLLÓ
Antoni Gaudí

Between 1904 and 1906, Gaudí radically remodelled the house of the industrialist Josep Batlló, giving it remarkable colouring and movement.
ⓘ

FUNDACIÓ TÀPIES
Lluís Domènech i Montaner

The Montaner i Simon publishing house was the first building in Eixample that combined open brickwork and iron in a new type of industrial architecture. Since 1984 the building has been the home of the Antoni Tàpies Foundation for promoting modern and contemporary art.
ⓘ

Shopping centre
The shops of the top labels are on
show in this unique display.

PASSEIG DE GRÀCIA

This avenue is an
open-air museum in
which some of the
most beautiful build-
ings in the world are
concentrated. Their
noble and intelligent
proportions, as Josep
Pla wrote, envelop
the passer-by.

LA PEDRERA (CASA MILÀ)

Antoni Gaudí

The forms of this
incomparable
building defy gravity
and the senses. Built
between 1906 and
1912 by Gaudí, it is
today an important
cultural centre run
by the Fundació
Caixa Catalunya. ❶

Barcelona is one of the most cosmopolitan cities in the world: extrovert, generous and open. Its Mediterranean essence is sensed in the vitality of its streets and the warmth of its people. A place full of surprises and nuances where each step provides us with a new promise and each glance reveals a mysterious secret.

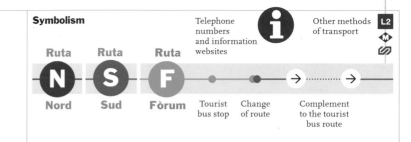

Symbolism

Ruta	Ruta	Ruta				
N	**S**	**F**	Tourist bus stop	Change of route	Complement to the tourist bus route	
Nord	Sud	Fòrum				

Telephone numbers and information websites

Other methods of transport

L2

Barcelona

Ruta **S** Sud   Ruta **N** Nord

L1 L3   L6 L7
Ⓜ Catalunya   Catalunya

Information point
Pl. Catalunya, 17
Basement

El Corte Inglés ▶

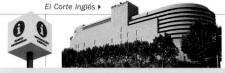

Aerobus

Plaça Catalunya

PLAÇA CATALUNYA

This square is the heart of Barcelona. It joins the old quarter of narrow streets with the grid of the Eixample area developed in the 19th century. It is the ideal starting point for any route.

MODERNISM

Movement at the end of the 19th century that corresponds to *Art Nouveau, Modern Style, Jugendstil,* etc.
It is characterised by the domination of the curve over the straight line, the taste for plant motifs, aesthetic refinement, movement and asymmetry.

CASA AMATLLER
Josep Puig i Cadafalch

CASA LLEÓ MORERA
Lluís Domènech i Montaner ▲

Goddess, Josep Clarà ▶

◄ *Meditation*, Josep Granyer
Flirt, Josep Granyer ►

ℹ **CATALONIA INFORMATION CENTRE**
Generalitat de Catalunya

Palau Robert houses an indispensable tourist office about all of Catalonia.

CASA COMALAT
Salvador Valeri Pupurull

Curious Modernist building with an original façade profusely decorated with ceramic motifs.

CASA DE LES PUNXES
Josep Puig i Cadafalch

Modernist building with a medieval air in which one can appreciate a certain Nordic influence

EGYPTIAN MUSEUM

Since 1993, Barcelona has had a museum exclusively devoted to the world of the Pharaohs. An excellent opportunity to discover the ancient Egyptian culture. ℹ

PALAU BARÓ-QUADRES
Josep Puig i Cadafalch

Home of Casa Asia, a body promoting contact between Spain and the Orient. ℹ

L5 **L2**
M
Sagrada Família

Information point
Pl. Sagrada Família

Temple of the
Sagrada Família
Guided visit

Schools

Museum

Sagrada Família

TEMPLE OF THE SAGRADA FAMÍLIA

Antoni Gaudí

Gaudí's most important work and the symbol of Barcelona in the world. In 1883 the architect took over the already started works and in his life was only able to complete the Nativity Façade, a veritable catechism in stone that achieves an amazing level of detail. Of unclassifiable style, this building is one of the most visited in the world, despite it being under construction. The museum is an absolute must visit with models and drawings of the entire project.
ⓘ

▲ Spiral stairway

▲ Cypress

▲ Central nave

HOSPITAL DE SANT PAU

Lluís Domènech i Montaner

Series of buildings in very innovative and advanced Modernist style compared to hospital design of the time.

Amongst its many details feature the sculptures by Pau Gargallo and the mosaics by Mario Maragliano.

GRÀCIA

Joined to Barcelona in 1867 via Passeig de Gràcia, this district of narrow streets, charming squares and bustling markets is one of the liveliest and most authentic spots, day and night.

CASA VICENS
Antoni Gaudí

This old summer residence, inspired by Arab and Mudejar architecture, is considered as the first important work by the architect.

CASA FUSTER
Lluís Domènech i Montaner

Modernist house from 1908. It is currently a luxury hotel catalogued as a Hotel-Monument.

PARK GÜELL
Antoni Gaudí

Park Güell is a public park although it was originally designed as a residential development along the lines of the English garden cities. The overwhelming architectural fantasies that we find in this place turn it into one of the most beautiful and unusual spots in the world. From 1906 Gaudí lived in the house that is today a museum dedicated to him One of the pavilions is the Park Güell Information Centre. ❶

PARC DE LA CREUETA DEL COLL

A park created from an old quarry which features the sculpture by Eduardo Chillida *Eulogy of Water.*

Tramvia Blau - Tibidabo →

COSMOCAIXA

A museum that provides an interesting view of science and recreates some natural habitats. The activities and exhibitions are based on interaction with the visitor. A fun way to learn. Ideal as a family activity.

ⓘ

EL PINAR
Enric Sagnier

Lit up at night, this house looks like an enchanted mansion that emerges from the Collserola hills.

LA ROTONDA
Adolf Ruiz Casamitjana

Modernist building of fine ornamental richness.

FABRA OBSERVATORY
Josep Domènech i Estapà

Astronomy centre that offers summer suppers with views of the stars.

TIBIDABO AMUSEMENT PARK

Situated on the highest peak of the Collserola range, this amusement park, known as the Magic Mountain, is the oldest in Spain. Some of its attractions, such as the automaton museum or the plane, date back to the early 20th century. ❶

Did you know that...?

The Tibidabo plane is a replica of the model that made the first Barcelona-Madrid flight.

COLLSEROLA PARK

An ideal spot to escape from the bustle of the city and a unique watchtower over Barcelona. ❶

COLLSEROLA TOWER
Norman Foster

This communications tower, 288 m high, was built to transmit the 1992 Olympic Games from Barcelona to the rest of the world. A lift goes up to a viewpoint at 115 m. ❶

Did you know that...?

The Foix confectionery shop was the property of the Catalan poet J.V. Foix (1893-1987)

◀ Crema catalana, a delicious dessert

SARRIÀ

Like Gràcia, Sarrià was a town in its own right until absorbed into Barcelona in 1921. In the old centre of the district there are outstanding buildings such as the 19th century Town Hall, the Modernist market, the church of Sant Vicenç or the Foix Confectioners.

BELLESGUARD
Antoni Gaudí

This building was erected over land where once stood the palace where the last King of Aragon was married in the 15th century. Aware of the symbolic value of the site, Gaudí paid his own particular homage to Catalonia and Catalan Gothic.

THERESAN COLLEGE
Antoni Gaudí

Gaudí found the first floor completed and had to fight against little money and time. The building is stone and brick, and its austere façade conceals beautiful architectural solutions such as the corridor of parabolic arches.

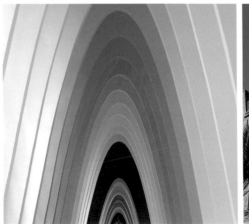

Did you know that...?

If you need good weather on a particular day you can make an offering of eggs to the nuns of the Order of St Claire who will pray for the good weather.

PARC DE L'ORENETA
Forest park with an enjoyable scaled-down railway.

Monestir de Pedralbes

MUSEUM-MONASTERY OF PEDRALBES
MHCB

Founded by Queen Elisenda, the last wife of Jaume II of Aragon, this series of 15th buildings represents the sobriety and elegance of Catalan Gothic. It features the frescos in the chapel by Ferrer Bassa and the royal sepulchre.

▲ *Birth, Ferrer Bassa*

▲ Dormitory turned into an exhibition room

Palau Reial - Pavellons Güell

GÜELL PAVILIONS
Antoni Gaudí

Pavilions watched over
by a fierce wrought
iron dragon. The
old pavilion stables
today houses the Real
Cátedra Gaudí, a study
centre. ❶

PALAU REIAL
The Royal Palace of
Pedralbes formed part
of the old Güell estate,
property of a powerful
Barcelona family of
industrialists. In 1924
the building was trans-
ferred to the Spanish
royal family to be used
as a residence during
their visits to the city.
It currently houses two
museums.

CERAMICS MUSEUM
The museum includes
an important Spanish
ceramic collection that
dates from the 11th
century until today. ❶

MUSEUM OF DECORATIVE ARTS
It houses a collection
of furnishings and
decorative items from
periods dating from
the late Middle Ages to
modern times. ❶

Futbol Club Barcelona

CAMP NOU

Opened in 1957, the stadium of Barcelona FC is one of the largest football stadiums in Europe. Going to a Champions League match or a classic derby against Real Madrid is an unforgettable experience. One hundred thousand voices support the blue and scarlet colours crying Barça, Barça, Barça! ❶

F.C.BARCELONA MUSEUM

From an old idea of the club's founder, Joan Gamper, in 1984 a museum was set up that brings us closer to the history of F.C. Barcelona. ❶

◀ *Pau Casals*, Apel·les Fenosa

L'ILLA

Rafael Moneo
Manuel Solà Morales

This architectural complex was, in its day, one of the most ambitious urban projects in Barcelona. Today it is one of the city's most important commercial centres.
ⓘ

TramBaix ▶

PLAÇA FRANCESC MACIÀ

Dedicated to the first President of the Catalan Government, the Generalitat, the square is one of the most important commercial and business areas in Barcelona.

AVINGUDA DIAGONAL

The name of this avenue should be interpreted literally. The Diagonal is a line crossing the whole of Barcelona joining the areas of the Llobregat and Besós rivers. Its final section has the name of Diagonal Mar.

Information point

Sants Station
Vestíbule

Tren	Procedència	Hora d'Arribada	Destinació	Hora de Sortida	Via
renfe Rodalies	L HOSPITALET	17.12	BLANES	17.13	2
renfe Rodalies	L HOSPITALET	17.19	UAB - MARTORELL	17.20	2
renfe Rodalies	CALELLA	17.21	L HOSPITALET	17.22	1
renfe Rodalies	L HOSPITALET	17.22	MATARO	17.23	2
renfe Rodalies	MANRESA	17.24	MARTORELL	17.25	1

PLAÇA DELS PAÏSOS CATALANS

This square is known as the first of the "hard squares" since it is predominately concrete. It is the antechamber of the large Sants station for long-distance and local train journeys.

PARC DE L'ESPANYA INDUSTRIAL

The park occupies the land of the old textile factory *La España Industrial*. Water plays a leading role in the formation of the setting as well as the sculpture of the dragon and the innovative lampposts.

L1
Ⓜ
Hostafrancs

L3 **L1**
Ⓜ
Espanya

Aerobus

Bus
Montjuïc
Turístic
Blue route
ⓘ

Information point
Plaça Espanya

Creu Coberta

Plaça Espanya

PARC JOAN MIRÓ

There used to be a slaughterhouse here –and it is also known as the Parc de l'Escorxador, Abattoir Park. It is the first example in the city of reusing an obsolete urban facility, and features the sculpture by Joan Miró, *Woman and Bird*.

CREU COBERTA

Commercial area that maintains the charm of the small local shop.

PLAÇA ESPANYA

The square was the entrance to the International Exhibition of 1929 held in Barcelona. The fountain in the centre, the work of Josep Maria Jujol, is inspired the classical forms of by Italian Baroque.

BARCELONA TRADE FAIR

The architects of the International Exhibition of 1929 belonged to the *noucentista* movement, which was inspired by the rationality of classical Italian aesthetics. This area is today the site of the biggest trade fair centre in Spain.

ⓘ

MAGIC FOUNTAIN

This work by Carles Buïgas, made in 1929, is a fanciful piece of hydraulic engineering that combines music, light and the rhythm of the water. A spectacle that still has the power to thrill whoever watches it.

CAIXAFORUM

The old Modernist Casaramona factory was rehabilitated by the Fundació la Caixa and since it was opened in 2002 has become one of the most dynamic cultural centres in the city. The entrance to the venue was designed by the architect Arata Isozaki. ❶

MIES VAN DER ROHE PAVILION
Mies van der Rohe

The German Pavilion was built for the International Exhibition of 1929. The work transformed the concept of luminosity and space in modern architecture. The current building is a replica of the original.
🛈

Morning,
Georg Kolbe ▶

Forum

POBLE ESPANYOL

During the International Exhibition of 1929, the Spanish Village was an open-air museum that grouped together all the architectural styles of the country through replicas of some famous buildings of Spain. Today it is a leisure centre with restaurants, bars, discotheques and concerts. ℹ

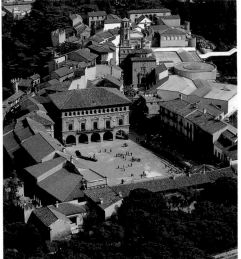

TEATRE GREC

In 1929, Ramon Raventós was inspired by the Greek theatre of Epidaurus to create this delightful open-air theatre where concerts and theatrical performances are held every summer.

CIUTAT DEL TEATRE

Centre dedicated to the world of the theatre. Of note is the dome of the Mercat de les Flors painted by Miquel Barceló.

ARCHAEOLOGY MUSEUM

The old Graphic Arts Palace of the International Exhibition of 1929 is today the Archaeological Museum of Catalonia.

NATIONAL MUSEUM OF ART OF CATALONIA
MNAC

The imposing National Palace, built for the Universal Exhibition of 1929 held in Barcelona, is the home of the most important museum in Catalonia. Its halls exhibit works that trace the history of art from Romanesque through to modern times. The Oval Hall is outstanding, 1,600 m² of space and a capacity for 1,200 people.
❶

THE PANTOCRATOR
From the church of Sant Climent de Taüll and painted around 1123, this Christ is considered as the most relevant work of Catalan Romanesque.

▲ Double sofa in the Casa Batlló, Antoni Gaudí

⬆ Odalisca, Marià Fortuny ▲ Mourners, Anonymous

◀ *Change*, Aiko Miyawaki

OLYMPIC RING

The Olympic Ring includes all the sports facilities built for 1992 Olympic Games and the city's old Olympic Stadium reformed in 1990.

Did you know that...?

They were going to hold the Popular Olympics in the Olympic Stadium, an alternative to the 1936 Olympic Games of Berlin. The outbreak of the Civil War stopped the event from talking place.

Censer ▶

ESTADI LLUÍS COMPANYS
Pere Domènech

This stadium, also known as the Olympic Stadium, was built in 1928 by Pere Domènech and is decorated with statues by Pau Gargallo. It was reformed for the 1992 Olympics.

PALAU SANT JORDI
Arata Isozaki

The most symbolic facility of the Olympic Ring. The roof of the pavilion, built with metallic net and glazed ceramic tiles, is a true symbol of Olympic Barcelona.

Torre Telefónica, ▲
Santiago Calatrava

PICORNELL SWIMMING POOLS
Open for anyone who wants an Olympic splash overlooking the city.

BOTANICAL GARDENS
Garden dedicated to Mediterranean flora possessing thousands of species from similar climates. ❶

FUNDACIÓ JOAN MIRÓ

Museum placed in a magnificent building by Josep Lluís Sert characterised by its large rooms, white walls and treatment of natural light. It includes most of the works by Miró, based on the use of colour and symbols. Interesting programme of temporary exhibitions. ❶

MONTJUÏC CABLE CAR

It connects the funicular station with the Alcalde viewpoint and Montjuïc castle.

MONTJUÏC CASTLE

The city was bombed from this citadel in 1842. It was also the gallows for members of the resistance against Franco.

The sardana is the traditional dance of Catalonia

❗ **Did you know that...?**

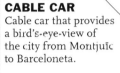

HELIPORT
Helicopter rides over Barcelona at a very affordable price. ❶

MONTJUÏC CABLE CAR
Cable car that provides a bird's-eye-view of the city from Montjuïc to Barceloneta.

WORLD TRADE CENTER BARCELONA
A business centre that includes a five-star restaurant and others with sea views.

COSTA I LLOBERA GARDENS
Botanical garden with great variety of tropical and desert plants. With a splendid cactus wood.

Bus Montjuïc Turístic
Red route ❶

L3 Ⓜ
Drassanes

Information point
Pl. del Portal de la Pau, s/n

Colom - Museu Marítim

MONUMENT TO COLUMBUS

Homage to Christopher Columbus, discoverer of America, by Cayetano Buigas for the Universal Exhibition of 1888. You can take a lift up to a small viewpoint providing beautiful views across the port and the Ramblas. ❶

GOLONDRINAS

Traditional boats offering tourist trips around the port, the breakwaters and the beaches of the city. ❶

MARITIME MUSEUM

Proof that Barcelona was an important commercial port in the Middle Ages is this Gothic building, the only medieval shipyard preserved in Europe. The Maritime Museum since 1980, it contains the royal galley that John of Austria captained in the Battle of Lepanto. ℹ

RAMBLA DE MAR

This walkway is a continuation of the Rambla into the sea. It leads to a former port area reconverted into a leisure centre.

In the 17th century the Moll de la Fusta was a beach and historians of literature believe that Don Quixote fought his last battle on it.

◀ *The couple*, Lautaro Díaz

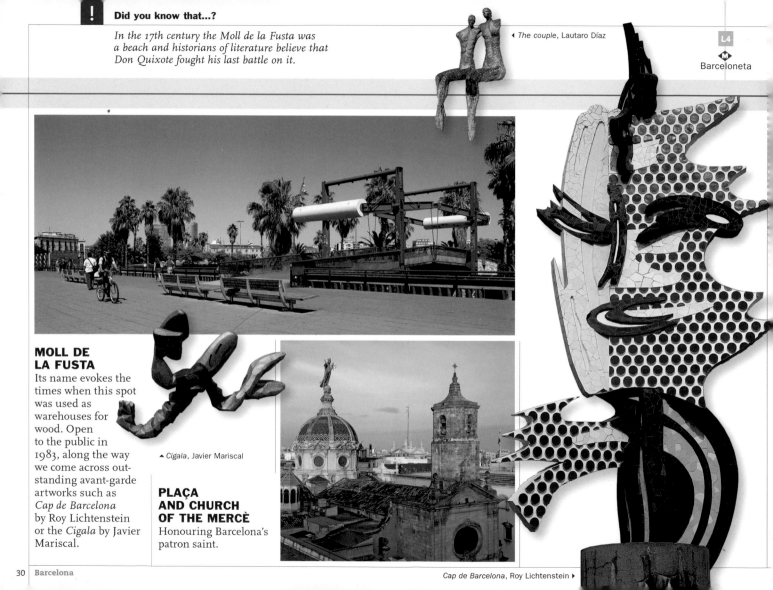

MOLL DE LA FUSTA

Its name evokes the times when this spot was used as warehouses for wood. Open to the public in 1983, along the way we come across outstanding avant-garde artworks such as *Cap de Barcelona* by Roy Lichtenstein or the *Cigala* by Javier Mariscal.

▲ *Cigala*, Javier Mariscal

PLAÇA AND CHURCH OF THE MERCÈ

Honouring Barcelona's patron saint.

Cap de Barcelona, Roy Lichtenstein ▶

MAREMAGNUM

Mare magnum is a Latin expression that means "big sea". And this is precisely what this immense architectural complex of Port Vell is, full of shops, restaurants and discos. Also open on Sundays. ❶

CINEMA IMAX

This cinema has a spectacular 27-metre long screen that shows films in Imax, Omnimax and 3D systems. ❶

THE AQUÀRIUM

One of the largest aquariums in Europe, it contains an important collection of Mediterranean species. ❶

FISHING PORT

It is still possible to find fishing boats moored in Barcelona and fishermen mending their nets in the sun.

BARCELONETA

La Barceloneta, an old fishing village, still conserves the hustle and bustle of the working class districts. It has some of the best beaches in the city and a seafront of over one kilometre. The terraces of the bars and restaurants are famous for their succulent seafood dishes.

MUSEUM OF THE HISTORY OF CATALONIA

Palau de Mar, a 19th-century warehouse, home to the Museum of the History of Catalonia.

TORRE DE SANT SEBASTIÀ

The Sant Sebastià tower was first in the concept of restaurant-viewpoint. Seafood cuisine at altitude.

Information point
Pg. Joan de Borbó, s/n
Almirall Cervera

BARCELONETA BEACH

*The wounded star,
Rebecca Horn* ▶

L4

M
Ciutadella-Vila Olímpica

PORT OLÍMPIC

Built for the 1992 Olympics, this sports port has over 800 moorings for small sailboats. The seafront has restaurants, shops, discos and nightclubs.

HOTEL ARTS
Bruce Graham

One of the most luxurious hotels in Barcelona.

GRAN CASINO

A casino alongside the sea with restaurants, bars and disco.

Marc, Robert Llimós ▼

◄ *Homage to Santiago Roldán*,
Eduardo Úrculo

▼ *David and Goliath*, Antoni Llena

SCULPTURES
The Vila Olímpica area
is home to some of
the most outstanding
sculptures of contem-
porary Barcelona.

Fish, Frank Gehry ▼

BIOMEDICAL
RESEARCH PARK
Manel Brullet
Albert de Pineda

The biggest science
building in southern
Europe.

TORRE
MARENOSTRUM
Enric Miralles
Benedetta Tagliabue

Home of Gas Natural.

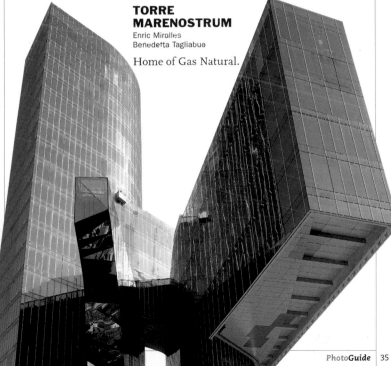

BEACHES

Barcelona's beaches are less than ten minutes from the centre. A privilege few big cities enjoy.

PARC DIAGONAL MAR

This park is one of the biggest in the city. It forms part of an urban recovery plan of old industrial sites in the Poblenou district.

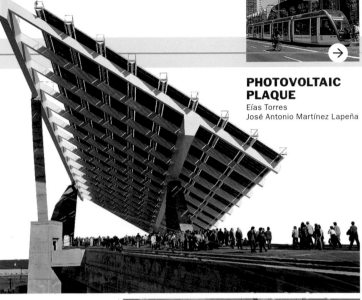

FORUM BUILDING
Herzon & De Meuron

Stunning building of the Forum of Cultures held in 2004, an event of a universal nature that promoted thought and dialogue about such important matters as cultural diversity, sustainable development and peace.

PHOTOVOLTAIC PLAQUE
Eías Torres
José Antonio Martínez Lapeña

BRIDGE
Mamen Domingo
Eduard Farré

INTERNATIONAL CONVENTION CENTRE OF BARCELONA
José Luis Mateo

Centre of International Conventions of Barcelona. The CCIB has 45 modular rooms and a capacity for 10,492 people. ❶

SKY HOTEL & RESTAURANT
Dominique Perrault

Building measuring 120 m in height by the author of the National Library of France in Paris.

PARC CENTRAL DEL POBLENOU
Jean Nouvel

Designed as a homage to the shade, its 55,600 m² are dominated by its willows and bougainvillea.

AGBAR TOWER
Jean Nouvel

Skyscraper 144 metres high that has changed the profile of Barcelona. Its shape is inspired by the eruptions of a geyser, Gaudian architecture and Montserrat mountain. The building is the headquarters of Aigües de Barcelona.

LA MONUMENTAL
Modernist bullring where
bullfights are held on some Sundays

→ **F**

TEATRE NACIONAL DE CATALUNYA
Ricardo Bofill

Building inspired
by the classical forms
of the Parthenon.
The centre, completed
in 1997, hosts a great
variety of established
shows from the world
of Catalan theatre
mainly.

L'AUDITORI
Rafael Moneo

The auditorium is the
permanent home of
the symphonic orches-
tra of Barcelona. The
building houses two
concert halls, dedicat-
ed to symphonic and
chamber music, and
also sometimes pop
concerts. It includes
the Music Museum.

ELS ENCANTS
The street market
of Els Encants is one of
the oldest in Europe.
Every week more than
50,000 visitors trawl
through the colour-
ful stalls in search of
a true bargain.

RAMBLA DEL POBLENOU
Poblenou has become one of the most attractive districts for visitors. Strolling along this avenue, which ends at the beach, one can discover the genuinely Mediterranean lifestyle.

POBLENOU
In the second half of the 19th century, Poblenou became the most important industrial area of Barcelona. In fact, the district was known as the Catalan Manchester and some of its old factories still stand proudly in memory of that period. Today the urban project of 22@ promotes the reuse of these buildings.

Can Felipa ▲

▼ Can Saladrigas

NIGHTTIME IN POBLENOU
Is one of the liveliest spots in the city. There are lots of bars and dance clubs among which feature Razzmatazz where they hold concerts and performances by the top DJs.

PLAÇA PRIM
A beautiful and hidden corner of the city where there is an excellent restaurant.

VILA OLÍMPICA

The Olympic Village was built to house the athletes of the 1992 Olympics.
It is a district with 2,000 homes with plenty of open spaces and gardens.

Telefónica Head Offices ◄

CEMETERY

Nineteenth-century necropolis that contains magnificent Modernist pantheons.

AVINGUDA ICÀRIA

Long avenue around which is formed the Olympic Village.

Pergolas, Enric Miralles ►

Did you know that...?

The mammoth of Parc de la Ciutadella was made at a life-size scale from a fossil discovered in Siberia in 1901.

L1 — Arc de Triomf   L4 — Ciutadella

Parc de la Ciutadella - Zoo

PARC DE LA CIUTADELLA

Ciutadella was a military fort from where the Barcelona people were "watched over" after the War of Succession in 1714. The demolition of the square in 1869 resulted in the space that housed the Universal Exhibition of 1888.

The umbrella lady, Josep Clarà ▶

PARLAMENT DE CATALUNYA

The Catalan Parliament was the old arsenal of the fortress.
ⓘ

Grief, Josep Llimona ▲

NATURAL SCIENCE MUSEUM

Known as the Castle of the Three Dragons, this battlemented neo-Gothic redbrick building is the only one conserved from the Universal Exhibition of 1888. Today it is the home of the Natural Science Museum.
ⓘ

SHELTER
Josep Fontserè ▶

HIBERNACULUM
Josep Amargós ◀

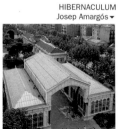

! **Did you know that...?**

For many years the zoo was home to Snowflake, the only albino gorilla in the world. Many of the zoo's gorillas are his descendents.

Modernist detail ▶

PARC ZOOLÒGIC

Opened in 1902, Barcelona Zoo contains species from all over the world. It has an excellent sample of African animals and the terrarium and dolphinarium are must visits.
ℹ

ARC DE TRIOMF
Josep Vilaseca

Open brickwork arch that was the entrance to the Universal Exhibition of 1888.

ESTACIÓ DE FRANÇA

Big engineering work from 1925 combining the modern metallic structures of the interior with the classicism of the façade.

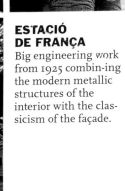

UPF LIBRARY

Old building that housed a water deposit which supplied the waterfall in Ciutadella Park. Today it is the library of the Pompeu Fabra University.

Pla de Palau

On the doors of Santa María del Mar homage is paid to the bastaixos, the porters who carried the goods from one place to another.

▲ Llotja de Mar

SANTA MARIA DEL MAR

Wonderful example of Catalan religious Gothic that here attains a level of sublime purity. The church dates from the 14th century and took 59 years to build, a record for the time. Of interest are the façade, the high naves inside and the effect of the light through the stained-glass windows.

EL PLA DE PALAU

Historically, the Pla de Palau was the main commercial square in Barcelona and the gateway for everything that came from the sea. It is surrounded by important buildings such as the Casa Llotja de Mar, the headquarters of the Barcelona Chamber of Commerce, Industry and Navigation.

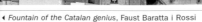

◄ *Fountain of the Catalan genius*, Faust Baratta i Rossi

FOSSAR DE LES MORERES
The trench of the soldiers who fought Philip V until the 11th of September 1714.

LA RIBERA
The name of this district gives an idea of the variety of trades that were plied here in the Middle Ages. In decline after the military defeat of 1714 by the troops of Philip V, the district was recovered with the construction of the Born market in 1876.

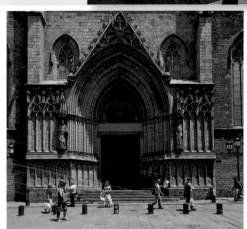

PASSEIG DEL BORN

The avenue, which today is a tourist centre surrounded by museums, restaurants and night spots, was once the spot where jousting tournaments were held. The inside of the Born market building houses the archaeological remains of the old Ribera district, destroyed by the troops of Philip V in the War of Succession.

CARRER MONTCADA

This street, full of shops, bars and art galleries, conserves an important series of palaces built between the 15th and 16th centuries, some of which have been turned into museums.

PALAU DELS
MARQUESOS DE LLIÓ
Textile and Clothing Museum ▶
🛈

PALAU NADAL
Barbier-Mueller Museum
of Pre-Columbine Art ▶
🛈

PICASSO MUSEUM

A series of palaces, most of them from the 14th century, were remodelled to house the museum dedicated to the Andalusian painter. In 1900 Picasso found in Barcelona the atmosphere he was looking for to develop his art. The museum is a worldwide reference for discovering the formative years of the painter.

PLAÇA SANT JAUME

Political centre of the city since Roman times. The square occupies the space that was once the Roman agora.

PALAU DE LA GENERALITAT DE CATALUNYA

This palace is the HQ of the Autonomous Government of Catalonia. The building conserves a Renaissance side façade. On the balcony of the main façade is St. George, Catalonia's patron saint. ⓘ

BARCELONA CITY HALL

The City Hall has been the home of Council since the 14th century. Architecturally, it alternates between the Gothic elements of the side façade and the neo-classical style of the main façade restore in the 19th century. Inside it features the magnificent Saló de Cent. ⓘ

Human towers, *castellers*, of Barcelona ▶

CARRER DEL BISBE

This is one of the busiest and most charismatic streets in Barcelona.

The neo-Gothic bridge that crosses it was built in 1928 by Joan Rubió i Bellver and is inspired by the Bridge of Sighs in Venice.

PLAÇA DE SANT FELIP NERI

Pleasant corner to relax in under the shade of the trees listening to the murmur of the medieval fountain. The Baroque façade of the 18th-century church is marked by the damage caused by the shrapnel and impact of bullets during the Civil War.

EL CALL

The name of Call was given to all the Jewish quarters of Catalan cities. This enclave of narrow streets was very prosperous in the 13th century. In the 14th century, the district was attacked and its inhabitants had to flee, persecuted by the Spanish Inquisition.

▲ Hotel Neri

TEMPLE D'AUGUST

Columns of the Roman temple to honour Emperor Augustus. 1st and 2nd centuries A.D.

Before Christmas in the Plaça Nova, the traditional Saint Lucy's Fair is held, dedicated to nativity scene accessories. The most popular figure is undoubtedly that of the **caganer**, *a young shepherd who is relieving himself.*

THE CATHEDRAL AND PLAÇA NOVA

The cathedral is the heart of the Gothic quarter. It was begun in the 13th century, but did not attain its current aspect until the 19th century, when Josep Oriol Mestres and August Font designed the façade according to neo-Gothic taste of the time.

Cloister ▾

BARCINO

Pedal taxi, an ecological alternative for visiting the city ▶

Plaça Nova ▲
Carrer del Bisbe ▼

MERCAT DE SANTA CATERINA

Enric Miralles
Benedetta Tagliabue

Local market rehabilitated with a bold multicolour roof that recalls, according to its authors, a still life of flowers and fruit.

Carrer de la Palla ▼

HISTORIC BUILDINGS IN THE PLAÇA DEL REI (MHCB)

Collection of historical buildings made up of the 13th-century Royal Palace with the Tinell Room, the chapel of Santa Ágata, the tower of King Marti, from the 16th century and Casa Padellàs. Beneath the square is a large archaeological site (I-VIII centuries). The visit to the buildings is run by the Museum of the History of Barcelona. ❶

FREDERIC MARÈS MUSEUM

Museum housing an interesting collection of archaeological items of the sculptor and traveller Frederic Marès. ❶

PALAU DE LA MÚSICA CATALANA

Lluís Domènech i Montaner

The Palau is a masterpiece of Modernism. Among its profuse ornamentation feature the sculptures, the muses of the stage and the fantastic skylight in the concert hall. ❶

PLAÇA RAMON BERENGUER

Enclave of Gothic buildings with remains of the Roman wall.

L1 L3
Ⓜ
Catalunya

Plaça Catalunya

↑ CASA BATLLÓ
LA PEDRERA

MACBA-CCCB

RDA. UNIVERSITAT

RAMBLA CATALUNYA

PASSEIG DE GRACIA

PAU CLARIS

RDA. SANT PERE

N

PELAI

Plaça de Catalunya ℹ

Aerobus ●

El Corte Inglés

PLAÇA URQUINAONA

FNAC

Plaça de Catalunya ℹ

Catalunya Ⓜ

Ⓜ Urquinaona

AV. PORTAL DE L'ÀNGEL

VIA LAETANA

Port Vell ↓

LA RAMBLA

↓ Catedral

Ⓢ

HORA OFICIAL

THE RAMBLA ON FOOT

LA RAMBLA

The avenue of the Rambla is the main artery of the old quarter. It is over one kilometre long until reaching the sea and is the first spot visitors discover, and who on setting foot on it, as if by magic, become citizens of Barcelona.

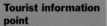

Tourist information point
Pl. Catalunya, 17
Basement

Tourist information, hotel booking, BCN Original gift article shop, Visits around the city and the surrounding area, and tickets for shows.

Alternative tourist routes:

Catalunya Bus Turístic
Montserrat, Sitges, Costa Brava, Dalí Museum...

Barcelona Walking Tours
Gothic Quarter, Picasso, Gastronomy, Modernism

Barcelona at night Bus Turístic
Magic Fountain and illuminated buildings

FONT DE CANALETES

The legend goes that anyone who drinks water from this hundred-year-old fountain always returns to the city. The *culés*, nickname of Barcelona FC fans, celebrate their titles around it.

CCCB

Albert Viaplana
Helio Piñón

The Charity House, and old 14th-century hospice, was remodelled to create the Centre of Contemporary Culture of Barcelona, an avant-garde space where cultural events are held.

ℹ

MACBA

Richard Meier

Museum dedicated to contemporary art and design. It has a collection among which feature the works of Tàpies, Brossa, Klee and Barceló. It also holds temporary exhibitions.

ℹ

The wave,
Jorge Oteiza ▶

EL RAVAL

The Raval district has historically been poor and marginalised. However, today it is one of the liveliest and most attractive spots of the city.

◀ *Cat,*
Fernando Botero

OLD HOSPITAL OF LA SANTA CREU

15th-century hospital that functioned until 1935. The 17th-century Convalescence Home can be visited, today the Institute of Catalan Studies.

LIBRARY OF CATALONIA

The magnificent vaulted hall of the old hospital houses the Library of Catalonia. ❶

BASILICA OF PI
Gothic style church built in the 14th and 15th centuries, with an imposing rose window.

Monument to Àngel Guimerà ▸

RAMBLA DE LES FLORS
This Rambla gets its name from the florists' stalls. Without doubt, the quintessence of the Rambla.

CHURCH OF BETLEM
Old Baroque Jesuit convent built in the late 17th or early 18th century.

PALAU DE LA VIRREINA
18th-century Baroque palace, home of the ICUB, the Institute of Culture of Barcelona. ℹ

PALAU MOJA
17th-century palace that houses the Department of Culture of the Generalitat.

The chef Ferran Adrià has his culinary laboratory close to the Boquería and is a regular customer of the market.

LA BOQUERIA

19th-century market considered one of the best in the world. It has an enormous variety of top-quality produce, as well as stalls specialising in exotic products such as mushrooms or... insects.

PLA DE L'ÓS

In the heart of the Rambla, facing the Boqueria market, we can walk over a work of art: the colourful mosaic created by Joan Miró in 1976.

Gran Teatre del Liceu ▼

GRAN TEATRE DEL LICEU

The Liceu features among the top opera houses of the world. The original building, from the 19th century, was destroyed by fire in 1994. Five years later it was reopened with *Turandot* by Puccini. ❶

▲ Cafè de l'Òpera

▲ Los Caracoles

CLASSIC BARS AND RESTAURANTS

Around the Rambla are authentic leisure venues that simply must be visited.

▲ London Bar

▲ Els Quatre Gats

▲ Pastís

▲ Grill Room

PALAU GÜELL
Antoni Gaudí

Built at the end of the 1880s for Eusebi Güell, a Catalan businessman who became Gaudí's main sponsor. ❶

SANT PAU DEL CAMP

The Visigoth elements of the front door show that the church existed before the 10th century. It had to be rebuilt in the 13th century according to the Romanesque model.

PLAÇA REIAL

Amidst palm trees, fountains and neoclassical façades is this arcaded square full of bars, restaurants and night spots. The lampposts are the work of Gaudí.

▲ Los tarantos   ▲ Jamboree

PLAÇA DEL TEATRE

Square facing the Teatro Principal, one of the oldest theatres in the city. There is a monument in honour of Serafí Pitarra, considered the founder of modern Catalan theatre.

CENTRE D'ART SANTA MÒNICA

Old 17th-century convent converted into a contemporary art centre.

WAX MUSEUM

Situated in a small 19th-century palace, the museum possesses a collection of wax figures of personalities from around the world.

THE RAMBLA ON FOOT

◀

TRIANGLE POSTALS

BARBIER-MUELLER MUSEUM OF PRE-COLUMBINE ART
Tel: 93 310 45 16
www.bcn.cat/cultura
Opening times:
from Tuesday to Friday, from 11 a.m. to 7 p.m.
Saturdays, from 10 a.m. to 7 p.m.
Sundays and public holidays, from 10 a.m. to 3 p.m.
Closed Mondays (except public holidays).
Free entry first Sunday of each month.
Services:
Shop/bookshop, cafeteria/restaurant, educational visits.

BARCELONA CITY COUNCIL
www.bcn.cat

BARCELONA CITY HISTORY MUSEUM (MHCB)
Tel: 93 256 21 22
www.museuhistoria.bcn.es
Opening times:
from 1 October to 31 May, from Tuesday to Saturday, from 10 a.m. to 2 p.m. and from 4 to 8 p.m. From 1 June to 30 September, from Tuesday to Saturday, from 10 a.m. to 8 p.m.
All year, Sundays and public holidays, from 10 a.m. to 3 p.m. Closed Mondays.
Services:
Shop, audio guide, guided visits, historical routes.

BOTANICAL GARDEN
Tel: 93 426 49 35
www.jardibotanic.bcn.es
Opening times:
April-June and September, from Monday to Friday, from 10 a.m. to 5 p.m.
Saturdays and Sundays, from 10 a.m. to 8 p.m.
July and August, from Monday to Sunday, from 10 a.m. to 8 p.m.
Free entry the last Sunday of each month.
Services:
Guided routes, media library, audio guide.

BUS MONTJUÏC TURÍSTIC
Tel: 93 441 49 82
Times:
From 26 June to 15 September, every day.
Rest of year, weekends only.

CAIXAFORUM
Tel: 93 476 86 00
www.fundacio.lacaixa.es
Opening times:
From Tuesday to Sunday, from 10 a.m. to 8 p.m.
Closed Monday (except public holidays). Free entry.
Services: Media library, bookshop, cafeteria/restaurant, educational workshops and activities.

CAMP NOU
Tel: 93 496 36 00
www.fcbarcelona.cat

CASA ASIA
Tel: 93 368 08 36
www.casaasia.es
Opening times:
From Tuesday to Saturday, from 10 a.m. to 8 p.m.
Sundays from 10 a.m. to 2 p.m.
Closed Mondays.
Services:
Media library, cafeteria.

CASA BATLLÓ
Tel: 93 216 03 06
www.casabatllo.es
Opening times:
from Monday to Sunday, from 9 a.m. to 8 p.m.
Services:
Visit with audio guide, shop.

CATALAN PARLIAMENT
Tel: 93 304 65 00
www.parlament-cat.net

CENTRE OF CONTEMPORARY CULTURE OF BARCELONA (CCCB)
Tel: 93 306 41 00
www.cccb.org
Opening times:
Tuesday, Thursday and Friday, from 11 a.m. to 2 p.m. and 4 to 8 p.m.
Wednesday and Saturday, from 11 a.m. to 8 p.m.
Sundays and public holidays, from 11 a.m. to 7 p.m.
Services: Bookshop/shop, cafeteria/restaurant, guided visits, educational service.

CERAMICS MUSEUM
Tel: 93 280 16 21
www.museuceramica.bcn.es
Opening times:

from Tuesday to Saturday, from 10 a.m. to 6 p.m.
Sundays and public holidays from 10 a.m. to 3 p.m.
Closed Mondays.
Free entry first Sunday of each month.
Services: Library, shop, visits with commentaries.

COLLSEROLA TOWER
Tel: 93 211 79 42
www.torredecollserola.com

COLUMBUS MONUMENT
Opening times:
from Monday to Sunday, from 9 a.m. to 8.30 p.m.

COSMOCAIXA
Tel: 93 212 60 50
www.fundacio.lacaixa.es
Opening times:
from Tuesday to Sunday, from 10 a.m. to 8 p.m.
Closed Mondays (except public holidays).
Free entry the first Sunday of each month.
Services: Cafeteria/restaurant, picnic area, shop/bookshop.

EGYPTIAN MUSEUM
Tel: 93 488 01 88
www.fundclos.com
Opening times:
from Monday to Saturday, from 10 a.m. to 8 p.m.
Sundays, from 10 a.m. to 2 p.m.
Services:
Library, shop, bookshop, guided visits.

FIRA BARCELONA
Tel: 902 233 200
www.firabcn.es

FREDERIC MARÈS MUSEUM
Tel: 93 310 58 00
www.museumares.bcn.es
Opening times:
from Tuesday to Saturday, from 10 a.m. to 7 p.m.
Sundays and public holidays, from 10 a.m. to 3 p.m.
Closed Mondays.
Free entry first Sunday of each month and Wednesday afternoons.
Services: Library, shop, cafeteria, guided visits.

FUNDACIÓ JOAN MIRÓ
Tel: 93 443 94 70
www.bcn.fjmiro.es
Opening times:
October-June, from Tuesday to Saturday, from 10 a.m. to 7 p.m.
Sundays and public holidays, from 10 a.m. to 2.30 p.m.
July-September, from Tuesday to Saturday, from 10 a.m. to 8 p.m.
Sundays and public holidays, from 10 a.m. to 2.30 p.m.
Closed Mondays (except public holidays).
Services: Bar/restaurant, library, shop, bookshop, guided visits.

FUNDACIÓ TÀPIES
Tel: 93 487 03 15
www.fundaciotapies.org
Opening times:
from Tuesday to Sunday, from 10 a.m. to 8 p.m.
Closed Monday.
Services: Guided visits, library and shop.